**candies,
cookies,
cakes
by the authors of
KIDS COOKING**

candies, cookies, cakes

Aileen Paul

by the authors of
KIDS COOKING

---

and Arthur Hawkins

Doubleday & Company, Inc., / *Garden City, New York*

ISBN: 0-385-03019-3 TRADE
       0-385-03066-5 PREBOUND
Library of Congress Catalog Card Number 79-79701

contents

4.75

a word to grownups

Were you chased out of the kitchen when you were a little kid, or were you allowed to share in the pleasure of cooking?

Whatever your own experience, having taught hundreds of children cooking, I've found that it is rewarding and creative and joyful for them. And boys and girls—measuring ingredients for fudge, stirring a batch of brownies, timing a spice cake carefully—acquire healthy appetites as well as healthy attitudes. Some important values become part of them as they work: values like sharing, assuming responsibility, and self-discipline in following the rules.

The rules for safety and procedure in the next chapter are important. It may surprise you that children, whose minds seem less cluttered than adults', abide by them easily. And when the rules and suggested steps are followed, there should be no problems.

Adults always want to know about cleaning up. And the answer is that of course the children should help clean up the kitchen after cooking. That, too, can be pleasant if there are clean sponges, ample towels, and nice-smelling liquid soaps to work with.

The right tools and the right equipment are important. The list on page 15, none of it expensive, should be helpful to your youngster.

a word to kids

Cooking is fun; it's a game. But as in all games there are certain rules to be followed. Since the rules of the kitchen are so important, you and a grownup should read these notes together.

RULES OF THE GAME

1. Turn handles of pots and pans you are using so that neither you nor anyone else will knock them off the stove or counter.

2. Use a dry pot holder when you place things in the oven or take them out. A wet pot holder is no protection against heat.

3. Use a paring knife (that's the little one that sometimes has a saw-toothed edge) for most of your cutting.

4. Use a wooden chopping board for cutting. Most counter tops scratch easily.

5. Use a wooden chopping board for hot pans.

6. Adults can be useful to you in the kitchen so, depending upon your age, let your "assistant" do the following:

    A. Turn on the oven or the burners of the stove.
    B. Stand by in case you need help when you are using the stove.
    C. Pour hot water for you when needed.

There's one rule that kids in my cooking classes have never broken, and I'm sure you won't either. Use the electric mixer or blender *only* when an adult is right there by you.

There are certain steps which must be taken:

Step 1. Read the recipe carefully. The recipes are chosen for ages seven to twelve, but what you can cook depends upon how much cooking you have done, and not upon your age.

Step 2. Check the list of ingredients to be sure you have everything you need *before* you start.

Step 3. Place together the ingredients and the equipment you will need.

Step 4. Place a damp sponge in a convenient spot to wipe up the spills that are bound to come. (Don't worry about them.)

Step 5. Make certain you understand the instructions. I have tried to be as brief as possible and to use only those cooking expressions that will be clear to you. Two that perhaps need to be explained are:

To *blend,* which means to mix several ingredients so that they appear to be one.

To *alternate* means to add some of one ingredient and then some of another until the step is completed.

about ingredients

1. **Flour**—all purpose presifted flour is generally used. It may be listed differently on the package: instantized, quick mixing, or similar words. If regular flour (not sifted) is used in baking, subtract 2 tablespoons per cup from amount called for. For cakes, flour is usually sifted. And sometimes cake flour (which is finely milled and made from soft wheat) is called for.

2. **Wheat germ**—the most nutritious part of the wheat kernel. It is taken out of white flour (and therefore most commercial white breads) because its removal makes bread last longer. Wheat germ can be bought at almost all grocery stores and can be added, following instructions, to many recipes.

3. **Shortening**—solid vegetable shortening, butter, or margarine. The last two can be bought in sticks which are measured.

4. **Sugar**—the one used every day is called granulated, but to keep recipes simple, we refer to it simply as sugar. Brown sugar is often used; and confectioners sugar is an important part of many frostings and candies.

5. **Syrup**—molasses, corn syrup, identified as light or dark. Some recipes call for maple blended syrup.

6. **Milk**—regular whole milk, skim milk, and non-fat dry milk, buttermilk, sour milk or cream, evaporated milk, and condensed milk (sweetened) in cans.
   (Other liquids in baking: coffee, water, fruit juices.)

7. **Eggs**—four sizes: small, medium, large, and extra large. If not shown in recipe, use medium.

8. **Baking powders**—complicated to explain but easy to use. Three types: tartrate, phosphate, double-action or SAS-phosphate are described on the label and sold under many brand names. Use phosphate or double-action for recipes in this book.

9. **Chocolate**—different varieties: un-sweetened, semi-sweetened, and sweet chocolate in bars divided into squares for easier use; chocolate pieces, called chips, bits, or morsels, made of semi-sweet chocolate; co-coa—ground chocolate with some fat removed.

10. **Flavorings**—liquid (vanilla, lemon, almond, and other extracts, oil of peppermint or wintergreen) or dried, such as spices (cinnamon, nutmeg, etc.). Grated lemon or orange rind also adds flavor.

11. **Nuts**—used for crunchiness, flavor, and health-giving qualities.

12. **Decorations**—candied fruits, flaked coconut, nuts, chocolate sprinkles, silver balls, and others.

about equipment

Most of the equipment you need is already in your kitchen, I'm sure. But here is a list of things that are especially needed:

baking pans, aluminum or glass. You have your choice of:

    8-inch or 9-inch round layer cake pans
    8-inch square pans
    12x8-inch pan
    13x9-inch pan

15

baking sheet (sometimes called cookie tin), 2, if possible.

cake racks, 1 long or 2 square ones
cake tester (or thin skewer, 3 or more
    inches long)
candy thermometer
cookie cutters
double boiler (water is placed in lower

part so that top rests about ½ inch above water)

electric mixer

grater

knife (a paring knife, the smallest of the set, will serve you well)

measuring cups

    1 nested measuring cup set (¼, ⅓, ½, and 1) makes measuring of solids easier

    liquid measuring cups (rim is above the top measuring line) of varying sizes, including 4-cup, which is most helpful (easier for small hands than dry measuring cups which have no rim)

measuring spoons, wooden, metal, or plastic

mixing bowls of different sizes

muffin pans

pot holders, 2

rolling pin

rotary beater (egg beater)

sifter

spatulas, broad rubber ones

    broad and narrow metal ones (if Teflon-coated pans are used, spatulas should be plastic)

wire whisk

wrapping paper—aluminum foil, wax paper, transparent Saran Wrap

about baking

Preheat Oven: Turn on the oven heat to the temperature given 15 minutes before baking. You probably need adult help for this step.

For accurate timing: Set timer when cookies or cakes are placed in oven, or write the time on a piece of paper.

Oven temperature for glass baking dishes should be set 25 degrees less than for metal ones.

17

To prepare cake pans:

1. Cut piece of wax paper to fit the bottom of pan.
2. Grease bottom and sides of pan lightly.
3. Place wax paper inside pan and grease paper lightly.

To prepare baking sheets:

1. Grease lightly, if called for in recipe.
2. Regrease each time used.

For even baking: Do not overcrowd cookies on sheet.

It is easier to make drop cookies the same size if you dip into dough with one teaspoon and use another teaspoon to push dough off on baking sheet.

Place baking sheet on top shelf in oven. Bake one sheet while getting the next ready, if you have two sheets.

Pour cake batter in equal amounts if using two pans. Place cake pan on shelf in middle of oven; if using two pans, stagger on two shelves.

Bake: Cookies until golden, not brown. Cookies are done when no impression is made when touched with finger tip.

Bake: Cakes until tester placed in center comes out clean and dry. Most cakes pull away slightly from sides of pan when done. If two pans are used instead of one, the time will be 5 to 10 minutes less.

After baking: Remove cookies from baking sheet immediately with spatula to rack, or as directed in recipe.

Leave cakes in pan on cake rack 5 to 10 minutes. Remove gently from pan and cool, right side up, on rack. Remove wax paper.

Cleaning: Scour and clean all baking pans and sheets thoroughly before storing. Use only for baking and not for other cooking if possible.

candies

20

candies you cook

PEANUT BRITTLE

CREAMY FUDGE

PEANUT MARSHMALLOW
   SQUARES

OLD-FASHIONED POPCORN
   BALLS

OLD-FASHIONED
   PEPPERMINTS

CHOCOLATE COCONUT
   BALLS

PULLING TAFFY

EASY LOLLIPOPS

helpful suggestions about candy making

1. Always make sure the temperature of the kitchen is *cool* when you're making candy. *This is important.*

2. *Follow the recipe exactly*—if you make even the smallest mistake in measuring, or in any other part of the recipe, you might ruin a whole batch of candy.

3. Allow plenty of time for candy making. It always takes a little longer than you think.

4. Be very careful to keep stirring candy whenever it is over heat. Many of the ingredients—milk, sugar, molasses, chocolate, etc.—are inclined to burn and stick to the bottom of the pan. *So stir and keep stirring.*

5. When melting chocolate in a double boiler, bring the water in the lower section to a boil, then turn down the heat, keeping the water just below boiling.

6. When beating hot candy, be very careful not to spill it on your hands.

7. Use a candy thermometer to tell you when the candy is done. Place the thermometer first into cold water and bring to a boil. Then place it in the candy and cook to the temperature called for in the recipe. After use, return the thermometer at once to hot water and cool gradually.

8. Doubling quantities in recipes is tricky because candy may boil over or cook too slowly. Better to make two batches.

9. When cutting candy into squares, wet the knife and the candy won't stick to it.

no-cook
peanut butter clusters

here's what you need

1 cup butterscotch chips

½ cup peanut butter

24

3 cups cornflakes or puffed rice

measuring cup (1-cup)

medium-sized saucepan

wooden spoon

wax paper

here's what you do

1. Put the butterscotch chips into a medium-sized saucepan and melt slowly over very low heat. Do not cook.

2. Stir in the peanut butter, a spoonful at a time.

3. Remove from the heat and stir in the cereal.

4. Carefully place spoonfuls on wax paper and cool in refrigerator until well set and firm.

no-cook fondant

here's what you need

$\frac{1}{3}$ cup corn syrup

$\frac{1}{3}$ cup softened butter or margarine

$\frac{1}{2}$ teaspoon salt

1 teaspoon vanilla extract

vegetable coloring

shredded coconut

chopped nuts

1 pound confectioners sugar

measuring cup (1-cup)

measuring spoons

mixing bowl

wooden spoon

chopping board

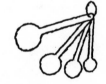

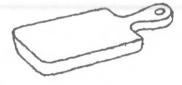

here's what you do

1. Put the syrup, butter or margarine, salt, and vanilla into the mixing bowl and blend well with the wooden spoon.

2. Add the sugar and mix well with the spoon. You can color with vegetable coloring, according to instructions on package.

3. Put the mixture onto the board and knead with your hands (make sure they are clean) until well blended and smooth. Here's how you do it: Pull the edges that are farthest away toward you, and push the nearest edges away from you. Do this three or four times, turn the board, and repeat.

4. Shape into balls, or roll out and cut into fancy shapes. You can roll balls in a bowl of shredded coconut or chopped nuts; for other shapes, just sprinkle on top.

27

no-cook chocolate peanut crunchies

here's what you need

¾ pound chocolate chips

¾ cup evaporated milk

1 cup Spanish peanuts

2 cups dry chow mein noodles
(or cornflakes)

measuring cup (2-cup)

medium-sized saucepan

mixing spoon

wax paper

here's what you do

1. Put chocolate into saucepan and melt slowly over low heat (do not cook). Stir in evaporated milk.

2. Stir in peanuts and noodles a little at a time until they are well coated with the chocolate mixture.

3. Carefully place spoonfuls of the mixture onto wax paper and cool until set.

no-cook
sugared nuts

here's what you need

1 cup sugar

$\frac{1}{4}$ cup water

$1\frac{1}{2}$ teaspoons cinnamon

$\frac{1}{2}$ pound almonds, peanuts, or any other kind of nuts

measuring cup (1-cup)

measuring spoons

medium-sized saucepan

ordinary tablespoon

wax paper or foil

here's what you do

1. Put sugar, water, and cinnamon into saucepan and bring to a boil over medium heat.

2. When mixture is clear and falls in heavy drops from spoon, add the nuts.

3. Stir until nuts are well coated, spoon onto wax paper or foil, and allow to dry.

no-cook chocolate marshmallows

here's what you need

$\frac{1}{2}$ pound semi-sweet chocolate cut into
   small pieces

6 marshmallows, cut into small pieces with
   scissors

$\frac{1}{2}$ cup chopped nuts

water

measuring cup (1-cup)

double boiler

wax paper

spatula

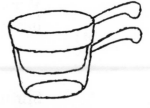

here's what you do

1. Boil water in the bottom part of the double boiler. Don't let the water touch the top pan.

2. Turn off the heat.

3. Place chocolate in the top part of the boiler. Stir until soft and gooey.

4. Add the marshmallows and nuts and mix well.

5. Spoon the mixture onto a sheet of wax paper and spread out thinly.

6. Cover with a second sheet of wax paper and flatten with a spatula.

7. Remove top sheet and cool in refrigerator. Break into pieces.

33

no-cook bon bons

here's what you need

2 tablespoons butter

⅛ teaspoon vanilla extract

10 tablespoons confectioners sugar

¾ cup nuts, very finely chopped

mixing spoon

tablespoon

cutting board

measuring cup (1-cup)

glass

here's what you do

1. Take butter out of refrigerator about half an hour before you are ready to start work so that it can soften.

2. Place the butter onto a cutting board and cream with a mixing spoon until it looks like whipped cream.

3. Measure ⅛ teaspoon of vanilla very carefully into a glass and then mix into the butter, a little at a time.

4. Add 1 tablespoon sugar to the butter and cream with the mixing spoon until sugar is thoroughly mixed in.

5. Repeat ten times, adding sugar a tablespoon at a time and blending each thoroughly with the mixing spoon—until all the sugar has been used up and is well blended into the butter.

6. Work the chopped nuts into the candy a little at a time.

35

7. Roll into balls, about 1 inch across, using your fingertips, and put into the refrigerator to harden.

Note: If you wish you may dribble melted chocolate over these bon bons.

peanut brittle

here's what you need

1 cup shelled peanuts

1 cup sugar

$\frac{1}{2}$ cup corn syrup

$\frac{1}{2}$ cup water

$1\frac{1}{2}$ tablespoons butter or margarine

small skillet

small or medium-sized saucepan

mixing spoon

measuring cup (1-cup)

measuring spoons

candy thermometer

shallow baking pan or cookie sheet

small amount of shortening to grease
   baking sheet

here's what you do

1. Grease shallow baking pan or cookie sheet.

2. Warm the nuts in a skillet over low heat for 5 minutes, shaking skillet occasionally to prevent burning.

3. Put sugar, corn syrup, and water into another saucepan.

4. Put a candy thermometer into the pan and bring mixture to a boil, stirring constantly.

5. Turn down the heat and cook until thermometer reads 290 degrees. Remove the thermometer.

6. Add the butter or margarine and the warm peanuts.

7. Mix well with a mixing spoon and pour onto the greased baking sheet. Spread around as thinly as you can.

8. When cool, break into irregular pieces.

creamy fudge

here's what you need

$\frac{2}{3}$ cup evaporated milk
   (undiluted—right out of the can)

1 cup sugar

1$\frac{1}{2}$ cups (9 ounces) chocolate chips

$\frac{1}{2}$ cup chopped walnuts

10 marshmallows, cut into small pieces
   with scissors

$\frac{1}{2}$ teaspoon vanilla extract

38 medium-sized saucepan

measuring cup (2-cup)

measuring spoons

8-inch square pan

small amount of butter to grease pan

spatula

ordinary table knife

here's what you do

1. Grease pan.

2. Put milk and sugar in the saucepan and bring to a boil over low heat, stirring all the time.

3. Continue to boil very slowly for exactly 5 minutes, stirring all the time to prevent sticking. This takes patience. If the heat is too high, the mixture will boil too fast and burn.

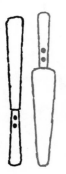

4. Remove from heat, add chocolate, nuts, marshmallows, and vanilla. Stir all the ingredients in well as you add them so that they become well blended. The mixture will get very stiff, and you may need grown-up help unless you are strong.

39

5. When the chocolate bits have melted and the mixture is creamy, spread in buttered pan, flatten with a spatula, and cool in the refrigerator until firm.

6. Cut into 1-inch squares with a wet knife.

peanut marshmallow squares

here's what you need

1 cup sugar

⅓ cup milk

½ cup marshmallow fluff

½ cup creamy peanut butter

½ teaspoon vanilla extract

measuring cup (1-cup)

small or medium-sized saucepan

candy thermometer

measuring spoon

mixing spoon

flat 8-inch square pan

small amount of shortening to grease
  square pan

ordinary table knife

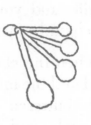

here's what you do

1. Grease the pan.

2. Put the sugar and milk in the saucepan with a candy thermometer and cook until thermometer reads 234 degrees. Remove the thermometer.

3. Add the marshmallow fluff, peanut butter, and vanilla.

41

4. Mix well with mixing spoon.

5. Pour the mixture into the greased pan.

6. Cool in refrigerator, then cut into 1-inch squares with a wet knife.

old-fashioned popcorn balls

here's what you need

1 cup dark or light molasses

1 cup sugar

1 tablespoon butter or margarine

2 quarts unsalted popcorn

42   measuring cup (1-cup)

medium-sized saucepan

candy thermometer

mixing spoon

wax paper

small amount of shortening to grease your
    hands

here's what you do

1. Put molasses, sugar, and butter or margarine in the saucepan with a candy thermometer and cook over low heat until thermometer reads 265 degrees. Remove the thermometer.

2. Add the popcorn, bit by bit, stirring well to coat all the kernels with molasses mixture.

3. Remove from heat and let cool for 15 minutes.

4. Grease your hands.

5. When cool enough to handle, shape into balls with your hands.

old-fashioned peppermints

here's what you need

6 drops oil of peppermint

1½ cups sugar

½ cup water

vegetable coloring, red and green

small glass

saucepan

mixing spoon

mixing cup (2-cup)

ordinary teaspoon

candy thermometer

wax paper

here's what you do

1. Measure 6 drops oil of peppermint into small glass. Be careful; this is very strong in flavor and too much will ruin your candy.

2. Put the sugar and water in a saucepan with a candy thermometer.

3. Heat, stirring constantly, until sugar dissolves into a syrup.

4. Boil until the syrup thickens and thermometer reads 265 degrees. Remove thermometer.

5. Add the 6 drops of peppermint.

6. Remove from heat (you might need grown-up help here) and beat with a mixing spoon until creamy. Add vegetable coloring according to instructions on packet.

7. Drop from a teaspoon onto wax paper, forming flat discs about 2 inches across. If the syrup becomes too thick, reheat it from time to time until it drops just right.

chocolate coconut balls

here's what you need

¹⁄₃ cup evaporated milk

³⁄₄ cup confectioners sugar

1 cup chocolate chips

³⁄₄ cup (about 8) marshmallows, cut into pieces with scissors

¹⁄₂ teaspoon vanilla extract

shredded coconut

small amount of shortening to grease baking sheet

small or medium-sized saucepan

measuring cup (1-cup)

measuring spoons

mixing spoon

baking sheet

here's what you do

1. Grease baking sheet.

2. Put evaporated milk, sugar, and chocolate in saucepan and bring to a boil. Keep stirring to prevent burning.

3. Turn down heat and cook 5 minutes, stirring all the time.

4. Add the marshmallows and vanilla. Continue cooking and stirring about 5 minutes longer or until mixture becomes stiff.

47

5. Spoon out onto greased pan and cool in refrigerator.

6. Form into walnut-sized balls by rolling with fingertips in the palm of your hand.

7. Roll balls in shredded coconut.

pulling taffy

here's what you need

1 cup molasses

1 cup sugar

1 tablespoon vinegar (any kind)

1 tablespoon butter or margarine

small amount of shortening to grease
platter and your hands

measuring cup (1-cup)

candy thermometer

measuring spoons

medium-sized saucepan

large serving platter

here's what you do

1. Grease the platter.

2. Put the molasses, sugar, vinegar, and butter or margarine in the saucepan with the candy thermometer and cook over low heat until mixture boils. Keep stirring.

3. Continue to boil until thermometer reads 265 degrees. Remove thermometer.

4. Pour onto greased platter. Keep folding the outer edges into the middle until candy cools enough to handle.

5. Grease both hands, pick up the taffy, and pull it. Here's the way you do it: take the taffy in both hands and pull into a thick rope. Put the ends together and pull again. Continue until taffy is stiff and light in color.

6. Pull into a rope ½ inch thick and cut into 1-inch pieces.

7. Cool completely.

49

easy lollipops

here's what you need

2 tablespoons grated orange rind—1 large or 2 small oranges

1½ cups pancake syrup (the maple-flavored kind is best)

2 tablespoons butter or margarine

¼ teaspoon salt

vegetable coloring

12 3-inch-long lollipop sticks

plastic or aluminum lollipop molds

small amount of shortening to grease molds

grater

measuring cup (2-cup)

measuring spoons

medium-sized saucepan

mixing spoon

candy thermometer

wax paper or foil

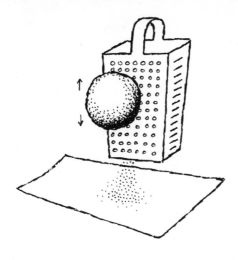

here's what you do

1. Grate orange rind onto a sheet of wax paper. Be careful not to grate your fingers!

2. Put syrup in saucepan with a candy thermometer and bring to a boil over medium heat.

3. Continue to boil without stirring until thermometer reads 265 degrees. Remove thermometer.

51

4. Stir in the butter or margarine, salt, grated rind, and vegetable coloring.

5. Grease the molds, place them on the wax paper, insert the sticks, and drop the syrup from a spoon into the molds. Let cool.

cookies

cookies easy to make

APRICOT PEANUT BUTTER DROPS

BROWNIES WITHOUT BAKING

CHOCOLATE BURRS

ORANGE CHOCOLATE CHIP COOKIES

52

NO-STIR COOKIES

CHOCO TREATS

HONEY DELIGHTS

QUICK COOKIES

cookies harder to make

53

apricot peanut butter drops

here's what you need

1 cup dried apricots

1½ cups peanut butter (smooth or
   crunchy)

¼ cup honey

1 cup flaked coconut

kitchen scissors or paring knife and chopping board

measuring cups (1- or 2-cup)

mixing bowl

mixing spoon, rubber spatula

ordinary teaspoon

paper plates or square of wax paper

here's what you do

1. Cut apricots into small pieces with kitchen scissors or chop with paring knife on board.

2. Measure and spoon peanut butter into bowl. Measure and add honey. Blend. (Blend means to mix thoroughly so that you cannot tell one ingredient from another.)

3. Stir in chopped apricots.

4. Drop by teaspoonful into flaked coconut spread on paper plate or wax paper.

5. Shape gently with fingertips into balls. Chill in refrigerator until firm.

brownies
without baking

Save a few of these for the grownups in your life. They'll like them.

here's what you need

1 cup walnuts

4 cups graham cracker crumbs

1 cup confectioners sugar

3 squares (3 ounces) unsweetened chocolate

1 cup plus 2 tablespoons evaporated milk

1 teaspoon vanilla extract

chocolate glaze if wanted (see Index)

small amount of shortening to grease pan

8 or 9-inch square pan

paring knife and chopping board

large mixing bowl

measuring cups (1- and 2-cup; 4-cup if available)

measuring spoons

saucepan

mixing spoon, rubber spatula, narrow metal spatula

here's what you do

1. Grease pan.

2. Chop nuts on board.

3. Measure and pour into mixing bowl: nuts, crumbs, and confectioners sugar. Stir.

4. Heat chocolate and evaporated milk over low heat, stirring constantly until smoothly blended. Remove from heat and add vanilla.

57

5. Gradually add to nut mixture, beating well. (If it becomes too stiff to stir, add small amount of additional milk.)

6. Spread evenly in pan. Glaze if you want.

7. Chill until ready to serve, about 6 to 8 hours.

chocolate burrs

A good recipe for a camping trip.

here's what you need

1 cup sugar

3 tablespoons cocoa

½ cup instant non-fat dry milk

2 tablespoons butter or margarine

¼ cup water

¼ cup peanut butter (smooth or crunchy)

pot holders

1½ cups quick-cooking oatmeal

1 teaspoon vanilla extract

measuring cups (1- and 2-cup)

measuring spoons

medium-sized saucepan

mixing spoon, rubber spatula, metal spatula

ordinary teaspoon

wax paper or foil

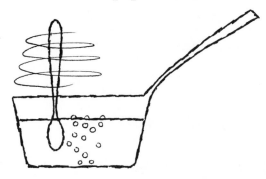

here's what you do

1. Measure and mix sugar, cocoa, dry milk, butter or margarine, and water in saucepan.

2. Place on medium heat. Bring to a boil and stir vigorously for 2 minutes. Immediately lower heat and simmer 2 minutes more.

3. Remove from heat and add peanut butter. Stir until melted.

4. Measure and add oatmeal and vanilla. Mix well.

5. Drop by teaspoonful on wax paper or foil.

6. Chill until firm.

orange chocolate chip cookies

A slight change with cookie mix gives quite a different taste.

here's what you need

1 package chocolate chip cookie mix

1 egg

2 tablespoons orange juice

small amount of shortening to grease baking sheet

baking sheet

large mixing bowl

cup (paper or styrofoam cup may be used)

table fork

mixing spoon, rubber spatula, metal spatula

2 ordinary teaspoons

cake rack

pot holders

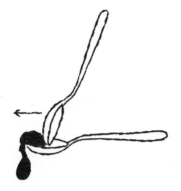

here's what you do

1. Preheat oven to 375 degrees.

2. Grease baking sheet.

3. Empty package into large bowl. Shake envelope of chocolate chips to remove clinging cookie mix and place to one side.

4. Break egg into cup. Add orange juice and beat with fork until blended.

5. Add to cookie mix and stir with spoon until thoroughly mixed. Add chocolate chips and mix again.

6. Drop by teaspoonful onto baking sheet using two spoons.

7. Bake 10 to 12 minutes.

8. Remove cookies to rack to cool, using metal spatula.

61

no-stir cookies

A good recipe for small hands because there is no beating, and yet it's a grownup recipe.

here's what you need

½ cup (1 stick) butter or margarine

1 cup graham cracker crumbs

1 cup flaked coconut

3 ounces chocolate chips

6 ounces butterscotch chips

1 can (14 ounces) sweetened condensed milk

12x8-inch baking pan

small saucepan

mixing spoon

measuring cup (1-cup)

pot holders

Condensed Milk
Butterscotch Bits
Chocolate Bits
Coconut
Graham Crackers

here's what you do

1. Preheat oven to 325 degrees.

2. Melt butter or margarine in sauce-pan over low heat.

3. Pour melted butter or margarine into baking pan, making certain that it covers bottom of pan.

4. Measure and add in layers: graham cracker crumbs, coconut, chocolate and butterscotch chips, condensed milk.

63

5. Bake 30 minutes.

6. Remove and cut into squares while still warm.

choco treats

Quick to prepare and ready for eating.

here's what you need

whole wheat or white bread (1 slice makes 2 rounds)

package of chocolate covered mint candies or chocolate chips

walnuts, pecans, or wheat germ

baking sheet or aluminum foil

paring knife and chopping board

2-inch cookie cutter or small juice glass

pot holders

here's what you do

1. Preheat oven to 300 degrees.

2. Chop nuts very fine.

3. Cut rounds of bread with cookie cutter or glass.

4. Toast in toaster until golden, not brown.

5. Place toasted rounds immediately on baking sheet or double thickness of foil.

6. Top with mints or chips and place in oven until chocolate melts.

7. Remove and sprinkle with chopped nuts or wheat germ.

8. Let cool slightly before eating.

honey delights

For easy-to-do bar cookies, they're delicious.

here's what you need

6 to 8 slices of day-old white bread

1 small orange

1 can (14 ounces) sweetened condensed milk

2 tablespoons honey

1 package (6 ounces) chocolate chips

small amount of shortening to grease pan

9-inch square baking pan

paring knife and bread board

measuring cups (1- or 2-cup)

grater

measuring spoons

mixing bowl

mixing spoon, rubber spatula, metal spatula

pot holders

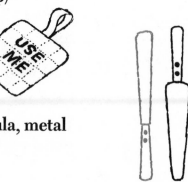

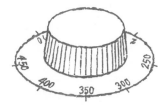

here's what you do

1. Preheat oven to 350 degrees.

2. Grease baking pan.

3. Remove crusts from bread with paring knife. Crumble slices, enough to measure 3 cups.

4. Grate orange, measure 1 teaspoon orange rind.

5. Slice orange in half and squeeze 2 tablespoons orange juice.

6. Put milk, honey, orange juice, rind, bread crumbs, and chocolate chips into bowl. Stir thoroughly.

7. Spread mixture in baking pan.

8. Bake 30 minutes. Cut into bars while warm and remove from pan before cool to prevent sticking.

67

quick cookies

here's what you need

½ cup chunky peanut butter

¼ cup honey

⅔ cup flaked coconut

2½ cups sugar crisp puffed wheat

large mixing bowl

measuring cups (1- or 2-cup)

mixing spoon, rubber spatula

paper plate or square of wax paper

here's what you do

Measure peanut butter, honey, and coconut into mixing bowl. Mix thoroughly.

Measure and stir in ½ cup cereal.

Spread remaining cereal on paper plate or wax paper.

Form balls of mixture with fingertips and roll in cereal on plate.

Chill in refrigerator until firm.

Note: You may substitute ⅔ cup cereal or ⅔ cup chopped nuts for coconut.

69

bar cookies

Bar cookies like these are easy, quick, and filled with health-giving things.

here's what you need

1 cup (2 sticks) butter or margarine

½ cup light or dark molasses

½ cup brown sugar

4 eggs

2 cups flour

1 cup wheat germ

2 teaspoons baking powder

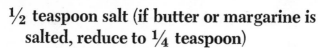

½ teaspoon salt (if butter or margarine is salted, reduce to ¼ teaspoon)

1 cup oatmeal

1 cup pitted dates

1 cup nuts

small amount of shortening to grease pan

13x9-inch baking pan

measuring cups (1- and 2-cup; 4-cup if available)

measuring spoons

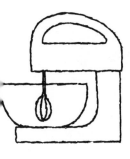

mixing spoon, rubber spatula

paring knife, chopping board

ordinary table knife or narrow metal spatula

pot holders

here's what you do

1. Preheat oven to 350 degrees.

2. Grease baking pan.

3. Beat butter or margarine in electric mixer until soft and creamy. Gradually blend in molasses and sugar.

4. Add eggs, one at a time, and beat lightly after each addition.

5. Measure flour, wheat germ, baking powder, salt, and oatmeal into 4-cup measuring cup (or small bowl) and mix gently with spoon.

71

6. Chop dates and nuts.

7. Add flour mixture, dates, and nuts to mixing bowl. Beat until blended.

8. Spread evenly in baking pan, using table knife or metal spatula. Bake for 30 minutes, or until done.

9. Cool in pan. Cut 1x2-inch bars.

molasses raisin bars

Another delicious bar cookie, almost as nutritious as the Bar Cookie on the preceding page.

here's what you need

¼ cup shortening

½ cup sugar

1 egg

½ cup light or dark molasses

2 cups flour

¼ teaspoon salt

¼ teaspoon baking soda

1½ teaspoons baking powder

½ cup milk

1 cup walnuts

½ cup raisins

small amount of shortening and flour for pan

13x9-inch pan

measuring cups (1- and 2-cup)

measuring spoons

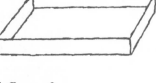

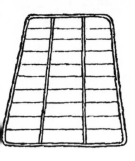

electric mixer with large bowl

paring knife, chopping board

pot holders

cake rack

here's what you do

1. Preheat oven to 350 degrees.

2. Grease and lightly flour pan.

3. Beat shortening in electric mixer until soft and creamy. Gradually blend in sugar.

4. Add egg, beat well.

5. Stir in molasses.

6. Measure flour, salt, baking soda, and baking powder into 2-cup measuring cup and stir gently.

7. Alternately add flour and milk to creamed mixture.

8. Chop walnuts, and stir nuts and raisins into batter.

9. Spread batter in pan and bake for 30 minutes, or until done.

10. Cool in pan for 5 minutes. Remove and place on rack.

11. When completely cool, cut into 4x1-inch bars.

marbled brownies

A few changes in a long-time favorite.

here's what you need

½ cup chocolate chips

½ cup peanut butter (smooth or crunchy)

⅓ cup butter or margarine

1 cup sugar

1 cup light brown sugar

3 eggs

1 teaspoon vanilla extract

2 cups flour

2 teaspoons baking powder

½ teaspoon salt (if butter or margarine is salted, reduce to ¼ teaspoon)

wax paper

13x9-inch baking pan

double boiler

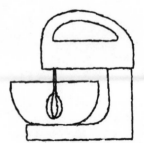

electric mixer with large bowl

mixing spoon, rubber spatula

measuring cups (1- and 2-cup)

measuring spoons

pot holders

ordinary table knife

here's what you do

1. Preheat oven to 350 degrees.
2. Grease and flour pan.
3. Melt chocolate in top of double boiler.
4. Beat peanut butter and butter or margarine in electric mixer until soft and creamy. Gradually blend in both sugars.
5. Add eggs, one at a time, and beat lightly after each addition. Add vanilla and blend.
6. Measure flour, baking powder, and salt. Stir gently to mix. Add all at once to butter mixture and beat until blended. (Batter will be stiff.)

7. Spread mixture in pan. Drop spoonful of melted chocolate over batter. With tip of knife, swirl chocolate into batter.
8. Bake for 30 minutes, or until done.
9. Cool in pan. Cut into bars of desired shape. Remove with metal spatula.

new brownies

*Brownie recipes are much the same. One has a little
more chocolate, another has a little less. But this one
is different because of magical wheat germ and the
taste is fantastic.*

here's what you need

1¼ cups flour

2 teaspoons baking powder

¾ teaspoon salt

2 cups sugar

¾ cup wheat germ

¾ cup (1½ sticks) butter or margarine

4 squares (4 ounces) unsweetened chocolate

3 eggs

2 teaspoons vanilla extract

1 cup nuts

Maple Frosting (see Index), if you would
like a frosting

small amount of shortening and flour for
pan

13x9-inch baking pan

measuring cups (1- and 2-cup, and nested
cups)

measuring spoons

electric mixer with small and large bowls

mixing spoon, rubber spatula

small saucepan

pot holders

narrow metal spatula

cake rack

ordinary table knife

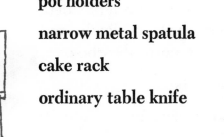

here's what you do

1. Preheat oven to 350 degrees.

2. Grease and lightly flour pan.

3. Measure dry ingredients into mixing bowl. Stir well to blend.

4. Melt butter or margarine and chocolate together in saucepan over low heat, stirring frequently. Remove from heat.

5. Beat eggs slightly in small mixing bowl; add vanilla.

6. Pour eggs into dry ingredients and beat on medium speed until blended. Add chocolate mixture slowly and continue to beat until absorbed.

7. Chop and add nuts.

8. Spread batter in pan. Bake 25 to 30 minutes.

9. Cool on rack. Spread with Maple Frosting, see Index. Cut in squares and remove with narrow metal spatula.

cut-out sugar cookies

The success of this recipe comes from chilling the dough. These cookies are fun to decorate with "silver" balls, halves of nuts, or chocolate sprinkles.

here's what you need

⅔ cup softened butter or margarine

⅔ cup sugar

2 eggs

1 teaspoon vanilla extract

2 cups sifted cake flour

1½ teaspoons baking powder

½ teaspoon salt (omit salt if butter or margarine is salted)

baking sheet

electric mixer with large bowl

measuring cups (1- and 2-cup)

mixing spoon, rubber spatula

small bowl

measuring spoons

fork, whisk, or rotary beater

sifter

wax paper

transparent Saran Wrap

rolling pin, bread board

cookie cutter

pot holders

broad spatula

cake rack

here's what you do

1. Preheat oven to 400 degrees.

2. Beat butter or margarine in electric mixer until soft and creamy. Gradually blend in sugar.

3. Break eggs into small bowl, add vanilla, and beat with fork, whisk, or rotary beater. Pour slowly into butter mixture, continuing to beat.

4. Sift cake flour into bowl or onto piece of wax paper, and then measure 2 cups. Add baking powder and salt. Resift. Pour into mixing bowl and continue beating until blended.

5. Form ball of dough and place on lightly floured transparent Saran Wrap. Fold airtight and place in refrigerator until chilled—about 1 hour. (You may chill dough in freezer in about 10 to 15 minutes.)

6. Remove and roll dough to ⅛-inch thickness on square of wax paper on board.

7. Cut into desired shapes with cookie cutter. Dip cutter lightly into flour each time you cut.

8. Place on ungreased baking sheet. Bake at 400 degrees for 8 to 10 minutes.

9. Remove to rack to cool, using spatula.

butterscotch thins

Chill dough before baking.

here's what you need

¹⁄₂ cup (1 stick) butter or other shortening

1 cup light brown sugar

1 egg

¹⁄₂ teaspoon vanilla extract

1¹⁄₂ cups flour

1 teaspoon baking powder

¹⁄₄ teaspoon salt (if butter is salted reduce to ¹⁄₈ teaspoon)

¹⁄₂ cup crushed bran flakes, Grape-Nuts Flakes, cornflakes, or chopped nuts

baking sheet

electric mixer and bowl

measuring cups (1- and 2-cup)

measuring spoons

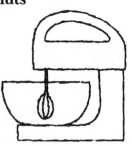

mixing spoon, rubber spatula

paring knife, chopping board (if you choose nuts)

transparent Saran Wrap

pot holders

broad metal spatula

cake rack

here's what you do

1. Beat butter in electric mixer until soft and creamy. Gradually blend in measured sugar.

2. Add egg and vanilla. Beat well.

3. Measure flour, baking powder, and salt together. Stir carefully to mix.

4. Slowly add flour mixture. Stir until thoroughly absorbed.

5. Stir in cereal or nuts.

6. Shape dough into two small rolls, about 2 inches in diameter. Smooth out all cracks. Roll airtight in transparent Saran Wrap. Chill in refrigerator until firm enough to slice with paring knife. (Dough can be chilled in freezer in approximately 10 to 15 minutes.)

7. When ready to bake, preheat oven to 425 degrees.

83

8. Take dough from refrigerator or freezer. Remove wrap. Cut in $\frac{1}{8}$-inch slices. Place on ungreased baking sheet and bake about 6 minutes, timing carefully.

9. Remove to rack and cool.

chocolate
peanut butter thins

This recipe was developed especially for my son Fred, who at a certain age would eat almost anything with chocolate in it. You can prepare these cookies easily without an electric mixer.

here's what you need

2 cups flour (may be half white and half whole wheat)

2 teaspoons baking powder

½ teaspoon salt

1 cup sugar

½ cup cocoa

½ cup vegetable shortening

½ cup crunchy peanut butter

2 eggs

⅓ cup milk

1 teaspoon orange extract

additional sugar (about ½ cup) in which to roll cookies

small amount of shortening to grease baking sheet

baking sheet

measuring cups (1- and 2-cup)

measuring spoons

electric mixer with large bowl

mixing spoon, rubber spatula

ordinary tablespoon

paper plate or square of wax paper

juice glass

pot holders

wide metal spatula

cake rack

here's what you do

1. Preheat oven to 400 degrees.

2. Grease baking sheet.

3. Measure flour, baking powder, salt, sugar, and cocoa into mixing bowl and blend.

4. Measure and add remaining ingredients to dry mixture. Stir until shortening and peanut butter are thoroughly absorbed.

5. Pour additional sugar on paper plate or wax paper.

6. Shape tablespoonfuls of dough into balls. Roll lightly in sugar on plate.

7. Place balls on baking sheet and press with bottom of glass until cookies are about ¼ inch thick.

8. Bake 8 to 10 minutes. Take care not to overbake.

9. Cool on sheet before removing cookies with metal spatula to rack.

frosty chocolate drops

A cookie that's heavenly to taste and *packed with healthful ingredients.*

here's what you need

2 squares (2 ounces) unsweetened chocolate

$\frac{2}{3}$ cup butter or margarine

$\frac{1}{2}$ cup nuts

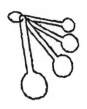

$1\frac{1}{2}$ cups flour

$\frac{1}{2}$ cup wheat germ

$\frac{1}{2}$ teaspoon baking soda

$\frac{1}{4}$ teaspoon salt (if butter or margarine is salted reduce to $\frac{1}{8}$ teaspoon)

½ cup each of sugar and brown sugar

1 egg

2 teaspoons vanilla extract

⅓ cup milk

small amount of shortening to grease baking sheet

Maple Frosting (see Index)

baking sheet

double boiler

measuring cups (1- and 2-cup; 4-cup)

measuring spoons

paring knife, chopping board

electric mixer with large bowl

mixing spoon, rubber spatula

2 ordinary teaspoons

pot holders

metal spatula

cake rack

here's what you do

1. Preheat oven to 350 degrees.

2. Grease baking sheet.

3. Melt chocolate and measured butter or margarine in top of double boiler (page 16). Remove from heat after chocolate is melted.

4. Chop nuts on board.

5. Measure flour, wheat germ, baking soda, salt, and sugars into 4-cup measuring cup. Stir lightly.

6. Break egg into large mixing bowl. Add vanilla. Beat well. Stir melted chocolate gradually into egg.

7. Add dry ingredients alternately with milk to egg mixture (alternately means first some of one and then some of the other).

8. Stir in chopped nuts.

9. Drop by teaspoonfuls onto baking sheet and bake 10 to 12 minutes, or until done.

10. Remove with metal spatula to cool on rack. Frost these with Maple Frosting (see Index), if you have time.

89

lollipop cookies

This recipe is fun. If you tire of putting straws in cookies, finish the cookies without them.

here's what you need

1 large or 2 small oranges

1 cup vegetable shortening

1½ cups brown sugar

2 eggs

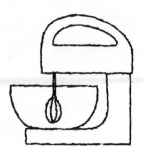

1½ cups flour

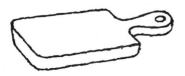

1½ cups quick-cooking oatmeal

⅓ cup wheat germ

1 teaspoon salt

½ teaspoon baking soda

1½ cups raisins

baking sheet

paring knife, chopping board

grater

electric mixer and large bowl

mixing spoon, rubber spatula

measuring cups (1- and 2-cup; 4-cup)

measuring spoons

2 ordinary teaspoons

paper drinking straws (*not plastic*)

pot holders

broad metal spatula

cake rack

here's what you do

1. Preheat oven to 375 degrees.

2. Grate orange, enough for 1 table-spoon rind. Slice orange in half and squeeze ¼ cup orange juice.

3. Beat shortening in electric mixer until soft and creamy. Gradually blend in sugar, eggs, orange juice and rind.

4. Measure flour, oatmeal, wheat germ, salt, and baking soda in 4-cup measuring cup and stir gently to blend. Slowly add dry ingredients to shortening mixture and continue beating until thoroughly mixed.

5. Stir in raisins.

6. Drop by rounded teaspoonfuls onto ungreased baking sheet.

7. Cut paper drinking straws in half. Push straw into dough to *center* of cookie.

8. Bake for 10 to 12 minutes, or until done.

9. Remove immediately from baking sheet with spatula and cool on rack.

western cookies

We have happy thoughts when we bake Western Cookies. We first ate them sitting on the porch in the clean and sweet-smelling air of western Nebraska with our good friends Helen and Bill Olson.

here's what you need

2 eggs

1 teaspoon vanilla extract

1 cup raisins

1 cup (2 sticks) butter or margarine

1 cup sugar

1 cup brown sugar

2½ cups flour

½ teaspoon salt (if margarine or butter is salted, reduce to ⅛ teaspoon)

1 teaspoon baking soda

1 teaspoon cinnamon

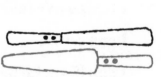

½ cup walnuts

2 cups quick-cooking oatmeal

small amount of shortening to grease baking sheet

baking sheet

small mixing bowl

table fork, whisk, or rotary beater

measuring spoons

measuring cups (1- and 2-cup)

electric mixer with large bowl

mixing spoon, rubber spatula

2 ordinary tablespoons

broad spatula

pot holders

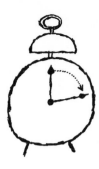

here's what you do

1. Preheat oven to 350 degrees.

2. Grease baking sheet.

3. Break eggs into small bowl. Beat with fork or whisk or rotary beater. Add vanilla and raisins.

4. Beat butter or margarine in electric mixer until soft and creamy. Gradually blend in both sugars.

5. Measure flour, salt, baking soda, and cinnamon into 2-cup measuring cup. Stir gently to blend.

6. Chop nuts.

7. Add half the flour slowly to butter mixture, beating on low speed. Add half the eggs and raisins. Continue to beat and add remaining flour and egg mixture.

95

8. Measure and add oatmeal and nuts. Mix thoroughly.

9. Drop by tablespoonfuls on baking sheet. Bake 10 to 12 minutes, or until done. *Do not overbake. This is a soft cookie, not crisp.*

cake

HELPFUL HINTS ON FROSTINGS, GLAZES, AND TOPPINGS

BUTTER CREAM FROSTING

CHOCOLATE FROSTING

GLAZE WITH VARIATIONS

CHOCOLATE GLAZE

MAPLE FROSTING

97

BROILED PEANUT CRUNCH TOPPING

CRUNCHY PEANUT FROSTING

WHIPPED CREAM TOPPING

helpful suggestions for cake mix

The instructions on the package are fairly easy to follow, but the way in which students in my classes work might be helpful.

here's what you need

1 package cake mix

eggs, as called for

small amount of shortening and wax paper
    for preparing pans

cake pans

small bowl

electric mixer with large bowl

measuring cup (1- or 2-cup)

mixing spoon, rubber spatula

pot holders

here's what you do

1. Remove eggs from refrigerator. Crack eggs into small bowl. (By doing that step *first*, eggs will lose some of their chill and cakes will rise higher.)

2. Preheat oven to 350 degrees, 325 degrees if using glass pans.

3. Grease and place wax paper in pan (page 17). Place cake rack and pot holders in convenient spot.

4. In large bowl combine cake mix, measured amount of lukewarm water as per directions, and eggs. Blend until moistened.

5. Beat length of time called for. Stop at halfway point and scrape bowl and beaters with spatula. (If beating by hand, use 300 strokes.)

6. Pour into cake pan or pans (even amounts if using two) ⅔ full.

7. Bake until done and cool according to instructions.

8. Additional nutrition may be gained by adding ½ cup wheat germ to cake mix and increasing water by ¼ cup.

cupcake cones

Great fun for a party!

here's what you need

1 package banana cake mix (1 pound, 2½ ounces)

eggs as called for on package

24 to 30 *flat-bottomed* ice cream cones

ingredients for frosting of your choice

100 muffin pans

small bowl

electric mixer with large bowl

measuring cup (1- or 2-cup)

mixing spoon, rubber spatula

cake rack

pot holders

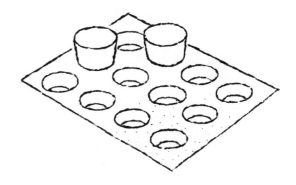

here's what you do

1. Preheat oven to 350 degrees.

2. Prepare cake mix according to instructions on package and suggestions in section "About Baking."

3. Fill ice cream cones three fourths full. Place each cone, as you fill it, in muffin pan standing upright. (Try to fill at same level for even baking.)

4. Place pan or pans in oven. Bake 20 to 25 minutes.

101

5. While cones are baking, prepare frosting and cover bowl.

6. Remove pans from oven (using pot holders) and cool cones on rack.

7. Frost in swirls.

gelatin poke cake

This cake is nice for the family. Allow plenty of time for baking, cooling, pouring gelatin, and chilling (about 3 hours' total preparation time).

here's what you need

1 package white or yellow cake mix (1 pound, 2½ ounces)

eggs as called for on package

pot holders

1 package fruit flavored gelatin (3 ounces)

Whipped Cream Topping

small amount of shortening and wax paper for pan

13x9-inch baking pan

small bowl

teakettle

electric mixer with large mixing bowl

measuring cup (1- or 2-cup)

cooking fork

small mixing bowl

cake rack

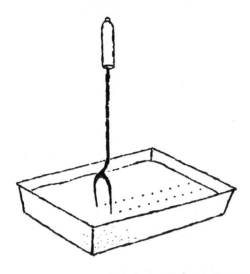

here's what you do

1. Preheat oven to 350 degrees.

2. Bring water to boil in teakettle.

3. Prepare cake mix according to instructions on package and suggestions in section "About Baking."

4. Cool cake in pan 15 minutes.

5. While cake is cooling, prepare gelatin by dissolving in 1 cup boiling water. You will need help from a grownup. Add 1 cup cold water and blend.

6. Make holes in cake every inch with cooking fork.

7. Slowly and evenly pour gelatin over cooled cake. Place in refrigerator for 2 hours to chill.

8. Prepare Whipped Cream Topping before serving and swirl over cake.

peanut butter
ice cream cake

The instructions are somewhat long, but the preparation is easy and the results are delicious.

here's what you need

1 package yellow cake mix (1 pound, 2½ ounces)

⅓ cup peanut butter (smooth or crunchy)

eggs as called for on package

1 quart vanilla ice cream

ingredients for frosting of your choice (see Index)

small amount of shortening and wax paper for pans

3 9-inch layer cake pans

small bowl

electric mixer with large bowl

measuring cups (1- or 2-cup and ⅓-cup)

mixing spoon, rubber spatula

aluminum foil, Saran Wrap

pot holders

cake rack

here's what you do

1. Preheat oven to 350 degrees.

2. Grease and place wax paper in *two* of the 9-inch layer cake pans (see section "About Baking"). Let ice cream stand at room temperature to soften.

3. Pour cake mix into bowl. Measure and add peanut butter. Mix on low speed until cake mix looks like coarse sand.

4. Continue with instructions on package for mixing, baking, and cooling.

5. Line other 9-inch layer cake pan with foil. (Let foil stand ½ inch above pan to make removal easier.)

6. Spread softened ice cream evenly in pan, cover tightly with Saran Wrap or foil, place in freezer.

7. Prepare frosting and cover to keep soft.

105

8. **To assemble cake:** Place 1 cooled layer on serving plate or platter.

   Remove ice cream from pan and place on cake layer, foil side up. Peel off foil. Top with second cake layer. Frost top and sides of cake.

9. If not served immediately, wrap tightly and place in freezer.

pineapple
upside-down cake

A pretty cake, and a yummy fruit and cake taste.

here's what you need

1 package yellow or white cake mix (1 pound, $2\frac{1}{2}$ ounces)

eggs as called for on package

$\frac{1}{8}$ pound ($\frac{1}{2}$ stick) butter

$\frac{1}{2}$ cup brown sugar

$\frac{1}{4}$ cup wheat germ (may be omitted)

1 small can pineapple rings ($8\frac{1}{4}$ ounces)

Whipped Cream Topping if you wish (see Index)

13x9-inch baking pan

small bowl

electric mixer with large bowl

measuring cup (1-cup)

mixing spoon, rubber spatula

pot holders

cake rack

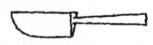

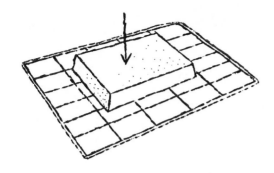

here's what you do

1. Preheat oven to 350 degrees.

2. Place butter in pan and melt in oven.

3. Remove pan from oven (remember to use pot holders) and sprinkle brown sugar and wheat germ in pan.

4. Drain liquid from pineapple rings and arrange rings in pan in a pattern.

5. Prepare cake mix according to instructions on package and suggestions in section "About Baking." Pour batter over pineapple rings and bake.

6. **To cool:** Turn pan upside down on rack for 2 minutes to allow syrup to drain into cake. Reverse pan and cool 10 minutes.

7. Remove carefully to serving platter.

8. May be served with Whipped Cream Topping.

107

vienna torte

From Austria in Central Europe comes the use of jam or preserves as a filling for cakes. It's an unexpected taste.

here's what you need

1 package devil's food or any dark chocolate cake food mix (1 pound, 2½ ounces)

eggs as called for on package

1 jar (12 ounces) apricot preserves

pot holders

Chocolate Glaze (see Index)

small amount of shortening and wax paper for preparing pans

2 9-inch layer cake pans

electric mixer with large bowl

measuring cup (1- or 2-cup)

mixing spoon, rubber spatula

small saucepan

cake rack

here's what you do

1. Preheat oven to 350 degrees.

2. Prepare cake mix according to instructions on package and suggestions in section "About Baking."

3. In small saucepan, heat apricot preserves to boiling, stirring frequently. Lower heat and simmer 5 minutes.

4. Let cool slightly while preparing Chocolate Glaze. Keep glaze warm over hot water to keep from stiffening.

5. Place cake layer on serving plate or platter. Spread with half the preserves. Top with other cake layer and spread remaining preserves. Let set 5 minutes.

109

6. Pour Chocolate Glaze over top of cake, completely covering preserves. Allow glaze to drizzle down sides.

7. Decorate top with Whipped Cream Topping if you wish.

no-sift chocolate cake

Try this cake and the one following and decide which you like better. As the name tells you, there's no sifting, and that means you finish more quickly. But sifting is fun, and perhaps you have time. There's very little difference in taste between the two. Oh yes, cakes like this used to be called "Busy Day Cakes."

here's what you need

2 cups flour

1½ teaspoons baking soda

1 teaspoon salt

¼ cup vegetable shortening

3 squares (3 ounces) unsweetened chocolate

1¾ cups sugar

½ cup sour cream

1½ teaspoons vanilla extract

2 eggs

ingredients for frosting of your choice (see Index)

small amount of shortening and wax paper to prepare pan

13x9-inch baking pan or 2 8-inch or 9-inch layer cake pans

tea kettle

electric mixer with large bowl

double boiler

111

measuring cup (1- and 2-cup)

measuring spoons

table fork

mixing spoon, rubber spatula

pot holders

cake rack

here's what you do

1. Preheat oven to 350 degrees, and put water to boil in teakettle.

2. Grease and place wax paper in pan (see section "About Baking").

3. Spoon flour gently into 2-cup measuring cup. Measure and add soda and salt. Stir in cup with fork to blend.

4. Melt shortening and chocolate in top of double boiler. Pour into mixing bowl.

5. Measure and add sugar and 1 cup boiling water to chocolate. Mix on low speed. If you are not old enough to handle boiling water, *let an older person do it for you.*

6. Measure and add sour cream, vanilla, and 1 egg. Beat on low speed until blended. Add second egg and beat until blended.

112

7. Stir in dry ingredients on low speed until moistened. Continue to beat, on medium speed, for about 1½ minutes, no more.

8. Pour into pan. Bake for approximately 30 to 35 minutes.

9. Cool as directed in section "About Baking" and frost as desired.

easy chocolate cake

The "sister" cake to the one before.

here's what you need

3 squares (3 ounces) unsweetened chocolate

2 cups cake flour

1 teaspoon baking soda

$\frac{3}{4}$ teaspoon salt

$1\frac{1}{2}$ cups sugar

$\frac{1}{2}$ cup vegetable shortening

$1\frac{1}{4}$ cups milk

1 teaspoon vanilla extract

2 eggs

small amount of shortening and wax paper
   to prepare pan

13x9-inch baking pan or 2 8-inch or 9-inch
   layer cake pans

electric mixer with large bowl

double boiler

sifter

measuring cups ($\frac{1}{2}$-cup, 1- or 2-cup, 4-
   cup)

measuring spoons

table fork

mixing spoon, rubber spatula

pot holders

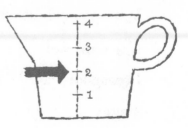

here's what you do

1. Preheat oven to 350 degrees.

2. Grease and place wax paper in pan (see section "About Baking").

3. Melt chocolate in top of double boiler.

4. Sift flour directly into 4-cup measuring cup until 2-cup line is reached.

5. Measure baking soda, salt, and sugar. Add to flour and mix thoroughly but lightly with fork.

6. Pour dry mixture into large mixing bowl and spoon in ½ cup shortening.

7. Measure milk and add vanilla. Pour ¾ cup (half the total amount) into bowl.

8. Beat 2 minutes on medium speed, no more.

115

9. Add remaining milk, unbeaten eggs, and melted chocolate. Beat 2 minutes on medium speed.

10. Pour into pans. Bake 30 to 35 minutes for layer cake pans and 40 to 45 minutes for 13x9-inch pan. Cool as directed in section "About Baking" and frost as desired.

chocolate carrot cake

WOW! Would you believe it, chocolate carrot *cake!*

here's what you need

1 package (6 ounces) chocolate chips

3 cups flour

1 teaspoon baking powder

1 teaspoon baking soda

1 teaspoon salt

1 teaspoon cinnamon

$\frac{1}{2}$ teaspoon nutmeg

$\frac{1}{4}$ teaspoon ground cloves

$\frac{1}{2}$ cup water

$\frac{3}{4}$ cup butter or margarine

1¼ cups sugar

2 eggs

1 cup grated carrots

1 cup raisins

small amount of shortening and wax paper to prepare pan

13x9-inch baking pan

electric mixer with large bowl

double boiler

grater

measuring cups (1- or 2-cup; 4-cup)

measuring spoons

table fork

pot holders

cake rack

here's what you do

1. Preheat oven to 350 degrees.

2. Grease and place wax paper in pan (see section "About Baking").

3. Melt chocolate in top of double boiler. Remove from heat when melted.

4. Grate carrots and measure exactly.

5. Sift flour directly into 4-cup measuring cup until 3-cup line is reached. Measure and add baking powder, baking soda, salt, cinnamon, nutmeg, and cloves. Mix thoroughly with fork.

6. Soften butter or margarine by beating with electric mixer. Measure and gradually add sugar and continue beating until blended.

7. Beat in eggs, one at a time.

8. Stir in melted chocolate alternately with water and flour.

9. Stir in carrots and raisins.

10. Pour into pan. Bake for approximately 35 minutes or until cake is done.

11. Cool as directed in section "About Baking." Frost with glaze or frosting of your choice in pan, or cut into squares and serve with Whipped Cream Topping.

oatmeal cake

Absolutely a unique taste. Try this cake, even if you don't like cooked oatmeal. It was a favorite at my aunt's farm in the West.

here's what you need

1 cup regular oatmeal

1 cup nuts

1 cup dates

2 eggs

¼ pound softened butter or margarine

2 cups brown sugar

1 cup flour

1 teaspoon baking powder

½ teaspoon salt

small amount of shortening and wax paper
  to prepare pan

13x9-inch baking pan

electric mixer with large bowl

measuring cups (1- and 2-cup)

measuring spoons

paring knife, chopping board

small bowl

fork or rotary beater

teakettle

pot holders

cake rack

here's what you do

1. Put approximately 1 cup water in tea kettle and bring to boil.

2. Measure oatmeal in 2-cup measuring cup. Pour boiling water into cup until it measures 2 cups. Let stand while you continue with the recipe. If you are not old enough to handle boiling water, *let an older person do it for you.*

3. Preheat oven to 350 degrees.

4. Grease and place wax paper in pan (see section "About Baking").

5. Chop nuts on chopping board. Dates may be chopped or cut with scissors.

6. Break eggs into small bowl and beat lightly with fork or rotary beater.

7. Soften butter by beating with electric mixer. Measure and gradually add sugar and continue beating until smooth.

8. Blend in eggs.

9. Measure flour and stir in baking powder and salt gently but thoroughly.

10. Add oatmeal and flour to mixing bowl, continuing to beat on low until thoroughly mixed.

11. Stir in chopped nuts and dates.

121

12. Pour into pan. Bake approximately 35 to 40 minutes.

13. Cool as directed in section "About Baking." Frost with glaze or frosting of your choice, or cut into squares and serve with Whipped Cream Topping.

golden cake

You may be the one child in twenty who does not like chocolate cake. If so, here's the right cake for you.

here's what you need

1½ cups cake flour

1 cup sugar

2 teaspoons baking powder

½ teaspoon salt

⅓ cup softened shortening

⅔ cup milk

1 teaspoon vanilla extract

1 egg

small amount of shortening and wax paper
   to prepare pan

2 8- or 9-inch layer cake pans or 13x9-inch
   baking pan

electric mixer with large bowl

sifter

measuring cups (1- or 2-cup; 4-cup)

measuring spoons

table fork

mixing spoon, rubber spatula

pot holders

cake rack

here's what you do

1. Preheat oven to 350 degrees.

2. Grease and place wax paper in pans (see section "About Baking").

3. Sift flour directly into 4-cup measuring cup until 1½ is reached.

4. Measure sugar, baking powder, and salt. Add to flour and mix thoroughly but lightly with fork. Pour dry mixture into mixing bowl.

5. Measure and add shortening to dry mixture.

6. Measure milk and add 1 teaspoon vanilla. Pour half into bowl.

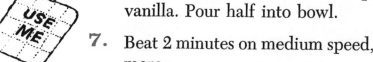

7. Beat 2 minutes on medium speed, no more.

123

8. Add remaining milk, unbeaten egg, and beat 2 minutes on medium speed.

9. Pour into pans. Bake 25 to 30 minutes for layer pans and 35 to 40 for 13x9-inch pan. Cool as directed in section "About Baking" and frost as desired.

spice cake

A delicious cake, and easy to change into a Raisin-Nut or Walnut Cake, as you will see.

here's what you need

1⅞ cups cake flour or 1¾ cups regular
   flour

¾ cup sugar

¾ teaspoon baking soda

¾ teaspoon salt

1 teaspoon cinnamon

½ teaspoon ground nutmeg

½ teaspoon ground cloves

¾ cup brown sugar

½ cup softened shortening

¾ cup buttermilk

2 eggs

small amount of shortening and wax paper to prepare pan

2 8-inch or 9-inch layer cake pans or 13x9-inch baking pan

electric mixer with large bowl

measuring cups (1- and 2-cup; 4-cup)

measuring spoons

table fork

mixing spoon, rubber spatula

pot holders

cake rack

here's what you do

1. Preheat oven to 350 degrees.

2. Grease and place wax paper in pans (see section "About Baking").

3. Sift flour directly into 4-cup measuring cup until $1\frac{7}{8}$ is reached.

4. Measure sugar, baking soda, salt, and spices. Add to flour and mix thoroughly but lightly with fork. Pour dry mixture into mixing bowl.

5. Measure and add brown sugar (sift if necessary to remove lumps), shortening, and buttermilk to dry mixture.

6. Beat 2 minutes on medium speed.

7. Add eggs and beat additional 2 minutes.

8. Pour into pans. Bake 30 to 35 minutes for layer cake pans and 40 to 45 minutes for 13x9-inch pan.

9. Cool as directed in section "About Baking" and frost as desired.

EASY CHANGES

Raisin-Nut Cake—Just before pouring batter into pans, fold in ⅓ cup chopped nuts and ⅓ cup raisins.

Walnut Cake—Just before pouring batter into pans, fold in ⅔ cup chopped walnuts.

helpful hints on frostings, glazes, and toppings

Frostings and glazes and toppings make a cake look attractive, help keep it fresh, and add or balance flavors. For example, if a cake is extra sweet, a less sweet Whipped Cream Topping might give the right taste.

Here's the way children frost cakes in my cooking classes.

For an oblong or 1-layer cake:

1. Brush crumbs away after cake has cooled.

2. Place a thin layer of frosting on sides and top as undercoating. Let harden, about 5 minutes.

3. Frost sides first, working with an upward stroke. Use generous amounts on narrow metal spatula.

4. Swirl top, finishing with scalloped edges to give a neat look.

For a 2-layer cake:

1. Brush crumbs away after cake has cooled.

2. Place first layer upside down on platter. Spread frosting almost to edge.

3. Top with second layer, right side up, and press down gently to bring frosting to edge.

4. Place thin layer of frosting on sides and top as an undercoating. Let harden, about 5 minutes.

5. Frost sides first, working with an upward stroke. Swirl top, finishing with scalloped edges.

There are many ways of decorating which are fun. You'll think of others, I'm sure.

Draw a clown face or a Jack-o'-Lantern with melted chocolate. . . .

Make a tree trunk and branches from chopped nuts. Fill branches with "silver" balls. . . .

Use little candies to make a raised edge or outline figures. . . .

Place small candy canes on top. . . .

chocolate frosting

Quick, quick, quick to do.

here's what you need

1½ cups chocolate chips

⅔ cup evaporated milk

3 cups confectioners sugar

measuring cups (1- and 4-cup)

heavy 1-quart saucepan or double boiler

mixing spoon, rubber spatula

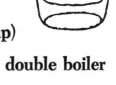

here's what you do

1. Measure chocolate chips and evaporated milk into saucepan.

2. Place over low heat and stir *continuously* until chocolate is melted and blended with milk.

3. Remove from heat. Add confectioners sugar, stirring until smooth. (Electric mixer can be used.)

4. If frosting becomes too thick, add few drops of evaporated milk.

Makes enough for 2-layer cake

butter cream frosting

The easiest and the best frosting, I think.

here's what you need

¼ pound (1 stick) softened butter or margarine

1 box (1 pound) confectioners sugar

⅛ teaspoon salt (omit if butter or margarine is salted)

1 teaspoon vanilla extract

3 to 4 tablespoons milk

electric mixer with large bowl (you can mix by hand)

measuring spoons

mixing spoon, rubber spatula

cake rack

130

here's what you do

1. Soften butter or margarine by beating with electric mixer (or by hand with sturdy mixing spoon).

2. Measure and add salt to sugar. Blend a third of the sugar with butter or margarine.

3. Measure and mix vanilla and milk. Add alternately to butter mixture with remaining sugar.

4. Beat until smooth. If you have measured accurately, the frosting should spread easily. If not, add milk in very small amounts.

Makes frosting for 2 layers or 1 oblong cake

HERE ARE CHANGES YOU CAN MAKE

1. Instead of vanilla, add 1 teaspoon any other flavoring such as almond extract, maple, artificial rum, or brandy flavoring.

2. Instead of vanilla, add 1 teaspoon grated lemon or orange rind and ½ teaspoon lemon or orange extract. Substitute 3 tablespoons lemon or orange juice and water if needed for milk.

3. For chocolate, add ⅔ cup cocoa mixed with sugar, and use hot water instead of milk.

4. For spice, add 1 tablespoon cinnamon to sugar and follow the recipe as given.

glaze with variations

Glazes are used for the same reason as frostings: to keep cake fresh, add flavor and prettiness. A glaze is thin, sometimes almost transparent, and becomes shiny when it hardens.

here's what you need

2 cups confectioners sugar

$\frac{1}{3}$ cup hot water

flavoring such as:

> 2 teaspoons grated lemon peel and $\frac{1}{2}$ teaspoon lemon extract
> > or
>
> 2 teaspoons grated orange peel and $\frac{1}{2}$ teaspoon orange extract
> > or
>
> $\frac{1}{2}$ teaspoon cinnamon
> > or
>
> $\frac{1}{4}$ teaspoon nutmeg

132

mixing bowl

measuring cup (1- or 2-cup)

measuring spoons

grater if needed

mixing spoon, rubber spatula

teakettle

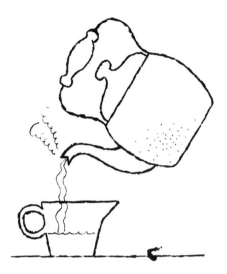

here's what you do

1. Put water to boil in teakettle.

2. Measure and pour sugar into mixing bowl.

3. Measure hot water from teakettle and pour over sugar. If you're not old enough to handle boiling water, *let an older person do it for you.*

4. Measure flavor of your choice (one of them) and add to sugar mixture.

5. Stir until smooth.

6. Pour slowly but immediately over cakes or cookies. If glaze thickens and cannot be poured, add small amount of hot water and stir again.

Makes about ¾ cup

133

chocolate glaze

Slightly different method than the preceding one.

here's what you need

2 squares (2 ounces) unsweetened chocolate

2 tablespoons butter or margarine

1 1/2 cups confectioners sugar

1/8 teaspoon salt if butter or margarine is
unsalted

4 tablespoons milk

heavy 1-quart saucepan

measuring cup (1- or 2-cup)

measuring spoons

mixing spoon, rubber spatula

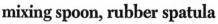

here's what you do

1. Unwrap chocolate and place in saucepan. Measure and add butter or margarine.

2. Melt on low heat, stirring continuously.

3. Remove from heat and stir in sugar (and salt if needed) gradually.

4. Mix thoroughly.

5. Heat milk (do not boil) and stir into chocolate mixture, a small amount at a time, until mixture is thin enough to pour. (Add a small additional amount of milk if needed for right consistency.)

6. While glaze is still warm, pour over cake or cookies.

Makes about ½ cup

maple frosting

*Another butter cream frosting. Especially nice on the
Frosty Chocolate Drops (see Index).*

here's what you need

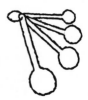

1½ tablespoons butter or margarine

1⅓ cups confectioners sugar

¼ cup maple blended syrup

⅛ teaspoon salt if butter or margarine is
   unsalted

mixing bowl

measuring cup (1- or 2-cup)

measuring spoons

mixing spoon, rubber spatula

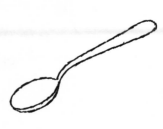

here's what you do

1. Measure butter or margarine into mixing bowl.

2. Soften butter or margarine by beating with mixing spoon (or electric mixer).

3. Measure and slowly add half of the sugar, blending well.

137

4. Add remaining sugar alternately with syrup; that is, first part of the sugar, then part of the syrup. Beat after each addition until smooth. Add salt if needed.

Makes about ¾ cup, enough for top of 1 layer. If more is needed, double the recipe

broiled peanut crunch topping

Broiled toppings have one advantage: they're delicious. They have one disadvantage: the pan has to be placed in the oven and removed with the heat on broil. With a hot oven like that, you'll need to get a grownup to help you.

here's what you need

¾ cup light brown sugar

½ cup smooth peanut butter

3 tablespoons softened butter or margarine

3 tablespoons milk

1 orange

⅓ cup peanuts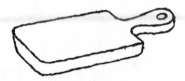

⅓ cup flaked coconut

mixing bowl

measuring cups (½-, 1-, or 2-cup)

grater

measuring spoons

paring knife

chopping board

narrow metal spatula or table knife for spreading

pot holders

here's what you do

1. Measure and pour into mixing bowl: brown sugar, peanut butter, butter, and milk. Stir until smooth.

2. Grate orange rind on piece of wax paper or small cutting board. Add to mixture.

3. Measure peanuts and chop on cutting board. Pour into bowl.

139

4. Add coconut and mix vigorously.

5. Spread mixture over top of cake while still in pan. (May be chilled until ready to serve.)

6. Broil as far from heat as possible until golden brown. Serve immediately.

crunchy peanut frosting

Nice for the Peanut Butter Ice Cream Cake (see Index) or any cake that needs a crunchy frosting.

here's what you need

1 can (16½ ounces) ready-to-spread vanilla frosting

¼ cup peanut butter (smooth or crunchy)

1 cup crushed peanut brittle

mixing bowl

measuring cups (¼- and 1-cup)

mixing spoon, rubber spatula

plastic bag

small hammer

here's what you do

1. Empty can of vanilla frosting into bowl.

2. Measure and stir in peanut butter.

3. Measure and crush peanut brittle by placing pieces in plastic bag and tapping gently with small hammer or sturdy object until brittle is very fine.

4. Spread frosting over cake. Sprinkle crushed peanut brittle over frosting.

   Makes about 2¼ cups, enough to frost a 2-layer cake or 1 oblong

whipped cream topping

Everyone has a favorite. I like Whipped Cream Topping on all varieties of cakes.

here's what you need

½ pint heavy cream, chilled

2 tablespoons sugar

1 teaspoon vanilla extract

electric mixer and bowl, or narrow deep bowl and rotary beater

measuring spoons

rubber spatula

narrow metal spatula for spreading

here's what you do

 1. Pour cream into bowl.

2. Beat until almost stiff. If using electric mixer, begin with low speed and increase to high, then low speed again as cream stiffens.

3. Add sugar and vanilla and resume beating until stiff.

Makes enough for top of cake. To frost sides, double recipe

Flavor can be changed by adding: **143**

  2 tablespoons cocoa and 2 tablespoons
     sugar
         or
  1 tablespoon instant powdered coffee
     and 2 tablespoons sugar
         or
any other extract or flavoring instead of
     vanilla and 2 tablespoons sugar

index